the field of WATERLOO

PAUL DAVIES

A PAN ORIGINAL

PAN BOOKS LTD : LONDON

First published 1970 by Pan Books Ltd,
33 Tothill Street, London, SW1

ISBN 0 330 02601 1

Printed by Sir Joseph Causton & Sons Ltd., Eastleigh

Contents

List of Maps

List of Illustrations

INFANTRYMEN AND PRIVATE OF THE 3RD
HUSSARS, KING'S GERMAN LEGION
   (From Charles Hamilton Smith: op. cit.)

GUNNER OF THE ROYAL HORSE ARTILLERY
   (From Charles Hamilton Smith: op. cit.)

PRIVATE OF THE 2ND, ROYAL NORTH BRITISH
DRAGOONS (THE SCOTS GREYS)
   (From Charles Hamilton Smith: op. cit.)

THE GREEN JACKETS: RIFLEMEN OF THE 60TH
AND 95TH REGIMENTS
   (From Charles Hamilton Smith: op. cit.)

WATERLOO CANNON
   (Courtesy of the National Army Museum,
   Sandhurst)

THE BROWN BESS

BELGIAN INFANTRY
   (From Richard Knötel: op. cit.)

PRIVATE OF THE 1ST REGIMENT OF LIFE GUARDS
   (From Charles Hamilton Smith: op. cit.)

PRIVATE OF THE 13TH LIGHT DRAGOONS
   (From Charles Hamilton Smith: op. cit.)

THE BATTLE OF WATERLOO
   (Detail from the painting by Sir William Allan, RA;
   courtesy of the Trustees of the Victoria and Albert
   Museum)

OFFICERS AND MEN OF THE IMPERIAL GUARD
   (From Moritz Rühl: op. cit.)

PRUSSIAN GUARD, INFANTRY AND JAGERS
   (From Moritz Rühl: op. cit.)

PRUSSIAN CAVALRY
   (From Moritz Rühl: op. cit.)

Acknowledgements

Grateful acknowledgement is made to Mr. John Mollo of the Historical Research Unit and Mr. K. Simmons, both of whom assisted in the preparation of this work.

The following publications were also consulted: *One-Leg: The Life and Letters of Henry William Paget, First Marquess of Anglesey, KG, 1768–1854* by the Marquess of Anglesey, FSA (Jonathan Cape Ltd., 1963); *A Guide to the Wellington Museum* by C. H. Gibbs-Smith and H. V. T. Percival (Her Majesty's Stationery Office, fourth edition, 1964); *Waterloo, Napoleon's Last Campaign* by Christopher Hibbert (The New English Library Ltd., 1967); *Waterloo* by John Naylor (B. T. Batsford Ltd., 1960; Pan Books Ltd., 1968); *History of the War in France and Belgium in 1815, containing Minute Details of the Battles of Quatre Bras, Ligny, Wavre, and Waterloo* by Captain William Siborne (T. and W. Boone, 1848); and *Men of Waterloo* by John Sutherland (Frederick Muller Ltd., 1967).

CHAPTER ONE

THE PROTAGONISTS

The Duke of Wellington

The Emperor Napoleon

THE DUKE OF WELLINGTON

Arthur Wellesley, 1st Duke of Wellington, was born in Dublin in 1769 and educated from 1781-4 at Eton. In 1786 he was sent to Pignerol's military academy at Angers and in the following year his brother, Lord Mornington, obtained for him a commission in the 73rd (Highland) Regiment. After the fashion of the time, he advanced through five different regiments and in September, 1793, he purchased the Lieutenant-Colonelcy of the 33rd Foot (later the Duke of Wellington's Regiment). In June, 1794, he sailed to the Continent and first saw action at Boxtel, where he distinguished himself by halting a French force which was driving back the Allies.

In 1796 he went to India as unofficial adviser to his brother, who had been appointed Governor-General. It was there that he built the foundation of his career, both as a soldier and a statesman. He took part in the invasion of Mysore and won victories over the Mahratta tribes at Assaye, Argaum and Gawilghur. He was put in charge of the civil administration of Mysore State and in September, 1805, when he returned to England, was promoted Major-General.

In 1806 he was re-elected to Parliament (he had previously represented the Irish constituency of Trim from 1790–5) and appointed Irish Secretary. Two years later he sailed for Portugal, and after winning the Battles of Rolica and Vimeiro was forced to take the blame for the unpopular Convention of Cintra and compelled to return to England. In 1809, following the death of Sir John Moore at Corunna, he was re-appointed to the command of the army and once more embarked for Portugal.

With his success against the French at Douro, Oporto and Talavera, he was raised to the peerage and in the years that followed consolidated his position in the Peninsula. He was elevated to Marquess in 1812, following his brilliant victory over the French at Salamanca, and in June, 1813, fought and won the great Battle of Vittoria, for which he was promoted Field-Marshal.

Further victories brought about the abdication of Napoleon and in May, 1814, when he returned to England, he was created Duke of Wellington. Later that year he was appointed Ambassador to France and, with Napoleon's return from Elba in the early months of 1815, Commander of the Anglo-Netherland and Hanoverian forces in Europe. After the French defeat at Waterloo he played an important part in the peace negotiations and retained his command of the Occupation Army until 1818, when he returned to England to re-enter politics.

He successively held the appointments of Master of the Ordnance and Lord Lieutenant of Hampshire, and he was Lord High Constable at the coronation of George IV. He was appointed Commander-in-Chief in 1827 and in January, 1828, became Prime Minister, which position he held until the Government fell in 1830. His period of office was a stormy one and brought him much unpopularity, and in the brief Peel administration of 1834 he served as Foreign Secretary. He was again appointed Commander-in-Chief in 1844 but from 1846 he ceased to take a prominent part in public life.

On September 14th, 1852, at the age of eighty-three, he died peacefully at Walmer Castle in Kent; he was accorded a State funeral and buried at St Paul's Cathedral on November 18th the same year.

THE EMPEROR NAPOLEON

Napoleon Bonaparte was born in 1769 at Ajaccio in Corsica and received his first commission in the artillery in 1785. He successfully repressed a Royalist rising in Paris in 1795 and was given command of the French army in Italy against the Austrians and by his victories at Lodi, Arcole and Rivoli in 1796 and 1797 compelled them to sue for peace. The Directory then accepted his plan to conquer Egypt as a half-way house to India but although he overran Egypt and invaded Syria, his fleet was destroyed by Nelson at the Battle of the Nile. He returned to France in 1799 and overthrew the Directory to establish his own dictatorship and, following his invasion of Italy and the defeat of the Austrians at Marengo, he successfully broke up the coalition which had been formed against France. Peace was eventually restored in 1802 and soon after, a plebiscite confirmed his Consulship for life. Another in 1804 granted him the title of Emperor.

War broke out again in 1803. A second coalition was formed against him and whilst he was prevented from invading England by British sea power, he drove Austria out of the war by his victories at Ulm and Austerlitz in 1805, and Prussia by his victory at Jena in 1806. Following the Battles of Eylau and Friedland, he formed an alliance with Russia at Tilsit in 1807.

He now attempted to ruin Britain with his Continental System which excluded British goods from Europe. Determined to enforce its operation he sent an army to Portugal and in 1808 placed his brother, Joseph, on the Spanish throne. Both countries rebelled, and with the arrival of English troops came the start of the Peninsular Campaign. Austria re-entered the war in 1809, only to be defeated at Wagram the same year, and when the Czar refused to support the Continental System, Napoleon invaded Russia and occupied Moscow. The ensuing retreat was catastrophic for the French army but it encouraged Austria and Prussia to declare war, which led to the French defeat at Leipzig. Napoleon was compelled to abdicate and was banished to Elba.

He returned to France in March, 1815, and embarked on his last campaign. With his defeat at Waterloo he returned briefly to Paris but was forced to abdicate a second time. He was exiled to St Helena, a lonely outpost in the Atlantic, and although there were plans to rescue him, drawn up by French exiles in America, he never left the island. He died in 1821 and in 1840 his body was re-interred in the Hotel des Invalides in Paris.

MARSHAL NEY

Michel Ney, Duke of Elchingen and Prince of the Moskowa, was born in 1769 and joined the French army in 1788. He rose from the ranks and served throughout the Revolutionary and Napoleonic wars, and he commanded the rearguard during the retreat from Russia. When Napoleon returned from Elba in 1815, Ney was sent to arrest him but instead deserted to him and was given command of the left wing of the army at Waterloo. He was subsequently shot for treason.

Marshal Ney

FIELD-MARSHAL VON BLÜCHER

Gebhard Leberecht von Blücher, Prince of Wahlstadt, was born in 1742 and took part in the War of Liberation against Napoleon which culminated in the French defeat at Leipzig in 1813. Although he was defeated by Napoleon at Ligny on June 16th, he was able to regroup his army to join Wellington to share with him the Allied victory over Napoleon at Waterloo on the 18th. He died in 1819.

Field-Marshal Prince von Blücher

THE EARL OF UXBRIDGE

Henry William Paget, Earl of Uxbridge (and later 1st Marquess of Anglesey) was born in 1768 and was in command of the British cavalry during the Peninsular Wars under Sir John Moore, and of the Allied cavalry at Waterloo, where he lost a leg. He succeeded his father as Earl of Uxbridge in 1812 and was twice Lord Lieutenant of Ireland before his death in 1854.

The Earl of Uxbridge

Marshal Soult

Louis XVIII

MARSHAL SOULT

Nicolas Jean de Dieu Soult was born in 1769 and entered the army in 1785. He served in the Revolutionary wars and was appointed Marshal of France in 1804 and Duke of Dalmatia in 1808. He held high commands in Spain throughout the Peninsular War and was Napoleon's Chief of Staff at Waterloo. From 1830 to 1834 he was Minister of War under Louis Philippe and again from 1840 to 1844. He died in 1851.

LOUIS XVIII

Born in 1755, the younger brother of Louis XVI, he was known as the Count of Provence until he assumed the title of King in 1795. He fled from France in 1791 and lived in exile until he obtained the throne in 1814. He fled again as Napoleon neared Paris but he returned after Waterloo to pursue a liberal and conciliatory policy until the assassination of the heir to the throne in 1820 led to a Royalist reaction. He died in 1824.

CHAPTER TWO

THE BEGINNING

On February 26th, 1815, less than a year after he had arrived in Elba, the Emperor Napoleon set sail for France once more, accompanied by an 'army' of 1,100 men. Confident that his former troops' loyalty to Louis XVIII would disappear as soon as they saw him, Napoleon had issued orders that on no account were his followers to open fire, and by reaching Paris without bloodshed he made any opposition to him virtually impossible. Royalist circles in the capital at first took the news of Napoleon's return lightly, believing that it would be an excellent opportunity to be rid of him once and for all, but as more and more of the civilian population gave him their support, so did the troops desert their officers and rally under his banner. Any resistance on the part of Louis was now out of the question and when he learned that Marshal Ney, who had been sent to arrest him, had in fact deserted to Napoleon, there was only one alternative open to him. In the middle of the night, on March 19th, he left Paris for Lille, close to the Belgian border. Shortly after, his ministers also followed him into exile.

A week before, at a conference attended by the Allied powers who had met in Vienna to rearrange the map of Europe, a manifesto had been issued which stated that since Napoleon had violated the convention which established him as independent sovereign of Elba, he had forfeited all claim to political existence and was henceforth to be considered an outlaw. Less than a fortnight later, England, Prussia, Austria and Russia pledged themselves to maintain an army in the field until Napoleon had been overthrown.

The Emperor realized as soon as he landed in France that war was inevitable if he was to retain his throne. The Allies had decided on a plan whereby three armies would converge separately on Paris, and even though the year of peace which had left them unprepared for war allowed Napoleon a breathing space, the situation for him was critical. Not only was he heavily outnumbered—conscription under Louis had been abolished and the army allowed to run down generally—he dared not order mobilization until his attempts to negotiate peace had definitely been rejected. What he did do, however, was order full production for the repair and manufacture of arms and uniforms and he instructed Marshal Davout, Minister of War, to purchase mounts for the cavalry.

On April 8th his peace proposals were rejected out of hand and mobilization was ordered. The days that followed were ones of considerable activity. Against a combined Allied strength of almost 700,000 men, Napoleon had little more than 180,000 he could use in the field. But he had determined his strategy: there was a chance that if he could strike first and successfully against Wellington and Blücher in the north, before they had time to concentrate their armies together, England might be out of the war for months to come. Belgium would then be his ally, enabling him to turn to the Russians and Austrians. If he could beat the former and pin down one of the Austrian armies by threatening Vienna, the other could be defeated so that total victory would be his. With every week that passed, the cards were turning in his favour.

In Brussels, where Wellington had arrived to take up his command on April 5th, the build-up of the English and

Prussian armies did not give the Duke much confidence. Blücher's force now totalled almost 120,000 men; his own, comprised as it was of Dutch-Belgians, Hanoverians and Brunswickers as well as English troops, contained a high proportion of recruits and soldiers who had no experience of battle, and he felt that only the Peninsular veterans of the King's German Legion could be relied upon in a crisis. But in the days that were to follow, the majority of them were to surpass his highest expectations and turn almost certain defeat into an outstanding victory from which Napoleon was never to recover.

Belgian cavalry of the Dutch-Belgian Army: *from left to right:* Officer of the 6th Hussars; Private and Officer of the 2nd Carabiniers; Officer and Private of the 4th Light Dragoons

Line infantry and cavalry of the French Army

CHAPTER THREE

THE BATTLES OF QUATRE BRAS AND LIGNY

Early in the morning of June 12th, Napoleon left Paris and travelled north to take command of his army. Both Blücher and Wellington were convinced that the offensive rested with them and Napoleon did all he could to make them continue to believe that he was preparing for their assault on the borders of France. He also wanted them to think that if he was going to advance, then he would attempt to sever Wellington's supply lines to the Channel.

Neither Allied commander had any idea that hostilities would begin so soon, so that when, on the evening of the 13th, reports started to reach Lieutenant-General von Ziethen, Commander of the Prussian 1st Corps, that the lights of bivouac fires were visible around Beaumont, he immediately notified Blücher, who ordered the 2nd, 3rd and 4th Corps to concentrate around Sombreffe. This was a bad mistake for Blücher had committed his army to an area within easy reach of a massed attack from the French. Napoleon had not decided which army he would attack first; beyond formulating his general plans, he had purposely waited until the best opportunity presented itself, but as soon as he heard of the Prussian concentration he determined to strike immediately in an attempt to end the campaign within forty-eight hours of its start.

Early in the morning of June 15th, French troops began to move across the frontier into Belgium. The characteristic three columns into which Napoleon divided his army advanced towards Charleroi. Soon after, Ney was appointed to the command of the left wing with orders to seize and occupy Quatre Bras, a vital cross-roads which controlled the com-munications between the English and Prussian armies. But for some reason, the Marshal halted his troops short of Quatre Bras; already Count de Grouchy, in command of the right wing, had engaged von Ziethen's forces and the Prussian general had fallen back to Fleurus. Ney's error enabled Prince Bernard of Saxe-Weimar to appear and entrench his Nassau battalions at the cross-roads, but had the French Marshal realized, he could easily have overpowered the enemy force.

But if Ney misunderstood the situation, so, too, did Wellington. Certain that if Napoleon was going to attack he would aim at cutting the Allied link to the sea, he did not at any time consider that the Emperor's intention was to separate the two armies. Not until midnight on the 15th, when the Duke and many of his officers were attending a ball given by the Duchess of Richmond, did he realize that he had been completely misled, by which time precious hours had been lost and totally inappropriate orders issued. Immediately he ordered his army to march on Quatre Bras. Napoleon had achieved his first objective: the Allied armies had been separated. With Blücher's troops at Sombreffe and, as he believed, with Ney at Quatre Bras, there was no possibility of them being able to join together.

The Marshal, however, had continued to do nothing and by so doing allowed reinforcements to reach Wellington until he found himself outnumbered. The situation at Quatre Bras on the 16th ultimately cost both sides many more casualties than was necessary and Napoleon his decisive victory over the Prussians.

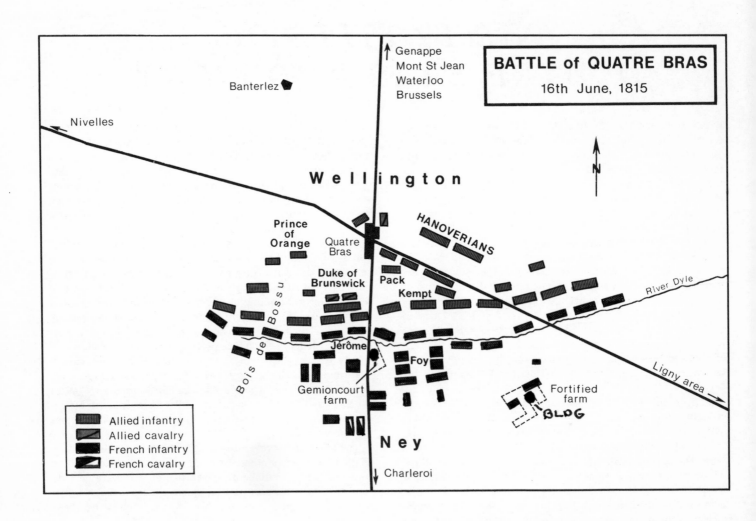

BATTLE of QUATRE BRAS
16th June, 1815

Genappe
Mont St Jean
Waterloo
Brussels

Banterlez

Nivelles

N

Wellington

HANOVERIANS

Prince of Orange

Quatre Bras

Duke of Brunswick

Pack

Kempt

River Dyle

Bois de Bossu

Jérôme

Foy

Ligny area

Gemioncourt farm

Fortified farm

BLDG

	Allied infantry
	Allied cavalry
	French infantry
	French cavalry

Ney

Charleroi

The Emperor's plan at Ligny was simple, although he still laboured under the mistaken impression that Ney had occupied Quatre Bras. He would contain Blücher's left flank and mount a tremendous assault which would crush the Prussian centre. A heavy attack both there and on the right would force Blücher to commit his reserves and then, with the whole army engaged, Ney would arrive from Quatre Bras to decimate, with the Imperial Guard, the greater part of the enemy force.

Shortly before three in the morning, the battle at Ligny began. A letter from Napoleon which arrived an hour later finally spurred Ney into action but the advance came to a halt; outnumbered by Wellington, Ney decided to wait until the 1st Corps, commanded by Lieutenant-General Count d'Erlon, reached him. But d'Erlon had also heard from the Emperor and had set off to join him. Delcambre, his Chief of Staff, returned to Quatre Bras to inform Ney of Napoleon's orders but Ney, who had been counting on these reinforcements to win the battle, countermanded them and instructed d'Erlon to return to Quatre Bras. By the time these further orders reached the 1st Corps, they were in sight of Ligny, having spent the entire day marching to and fro between the two battlefields.

By this time, Ney had committed his entire force, with the exception of Lieutenant-General Kellermann's cuirassiers and the Cavalry of the Guard. Heavily outnumbered though they were, Ney ordered Kellermann to charge; they stormed through the ranks of the 69th and succeeded in displacing the 33rd until they arrived at Quatre Bras itself. But here the attack came to an end for there was no support to distract the enemy, and the outcome of Kellermann's heroic charge was to weaken the hard-pressed French line. Slowly they began to fall back until at nightfall both armies found themselves occupying the ground they had held at midday.

Because of Ney's obstinacy, Napoleon was forced to fight at Ligny without d'Erlon's Corps. Yet he still managed to deliver a crippling blow to Blücher's army, for its lack of experience in comparison to the veteran French troops forced the Prussian Field-Marshal to commit his reserves whilst the Imperial Guard remained intact behind the French lines.

Confusion broke out when it was reported to Napoleon that a mysterious column was approaching the French left. It was in fact d'Erlon, but Blücher took advantage of the muddle to launch a final all-out attack. The French held and, two hours later than he intended, Napoleon ordered the Guard to advance. The Prussian centre collapsed at the onslaught and the remains of the divisions which had defended the centre withdrew in chaos to Sombreffe. Darkness brought the French advance to a halt; without doubt they had won the day, but had d'Erlon's Corps been at Sombreffe as the Prussians retreated from the Guards' assault, Blücher's army would have collapsed completely. Nevertheless, the way was left open for Napoleon to attack Wellington; what he did not, and never would, envisage was that Blücher would be able to recover his army in time to reach and be of assistance to the Duke at Waterloo on the 18th.

An OFFICER & PRIVATE of the 52.d REGT of LT INFANTRY.

Officer and Private of the 52nd Regiment, Line Infantry

BATTALION INFANTRY.
6TH or 1ST WARWICKSHIRE REGIMENT.
23RD or ROYAL WELSH FUSILEERS.

Privates of the 23rd, or Royal Welsh Fusiliers, and 1st Warwickshire Regiment (which did not take part in the battle)

CHAPTER FOUR

JUNE 17TH

Soon after midnight on the morning of June 17th, reports started to filter through to Napoleon that the Prussians were retreating towards Liège and Namur; this was, in fact, the first of many misunderstandings which were to occur that day, for the main body of Blücher's army was about to march in a completely different direction, to Wavre. Had Napoleon acted with the thoroughness he normally exhibited after a battle, this error might have been corrected and others avoided altogether, but instead of ordering his cavalry to cover the Prussian retreat, he merely set out on a tour of the battlefield.

What the Emperor should have done was to exploit the severing of the Allied armies; a despatch to Ney suggests that he believed Wellington to be withdrawing his troops from Quatre Bras and it would have been simple for him to send out a detachment to ensure that Blücher retreated away from the Duke, whilst he himself immediately engaged the English in battle.

Once Wellington received the news of Blücher's defeat, Ney's inactivity enabled him to retreat without any interference from the French. The Marshal, still believing that he had the whole English army before him, had not even bothered to send out a patrol to reconnoitre the situation. Wellington ordered his men to fall back on Waterloo and he told a Prussian aide to inform his Commander that, provided he could rely on the assistance of at least one Prussian Corps, he would engage the enemy there.

In the meantime, Napoleon continued to display an astonishing indifference to the state of affairs in front of him. When finally he did wake up to the situation, he realized that both Blücher and Wellington had been given an opportunity to evade defeat. Immediately he began to rectify the errors he had made, galloping to the head of the column to lead the pursuit against the English. But the weather was also against him. Heavy rain made it impossible for the French to advance across the open countryside and they were compelled to use the single crowded road. Moreover, many of the troops were far behind him and when he eventually encamped for the night, a great number of them continued to arrive well into the early hours of the morning.

Wellington established his headquarters in the village of Waterloo and waited for word from Blücher, for unless he was promised the support he wanted he intended to retreat still farther. Shortly after two o'clock on the 18th, a letter reached him: General Count Bülow von Dennewitz's 4th Corps would march towards Waterloo at daybreak, followed soon after by the 1st and 2nd Corps. Wellington decided to offer battle next morning.

Napoleon, on the other hand, still refused to believe that Blücher was in a position to join the English . . .

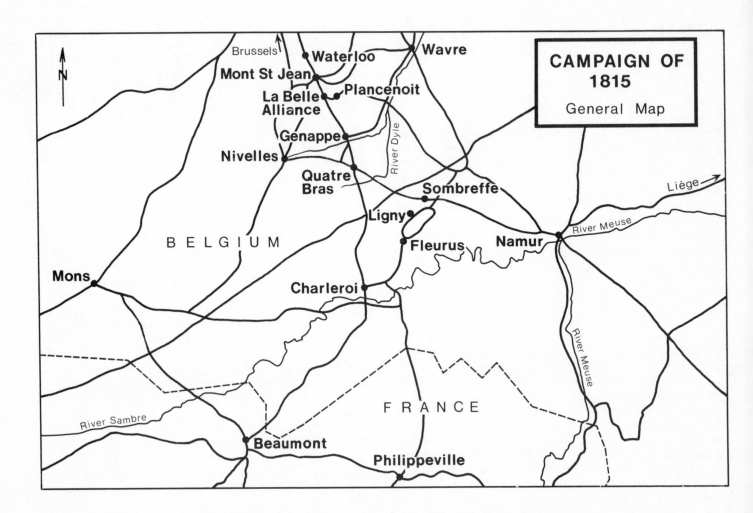

CAMPAIGN OF 1815

General Map

N

Brussels
Waterloo
Wavre
Mont St Jean
Plancenoit
La Belle Alliance
Genappe
Nivelles
Quatre Bras
Sombreffe
Liège
Ligny
Fleurus
River Meuse
Namur
BELGIUM
River Dyle
Mons
Charleroi
FRANCE
River Meuse
River Sambre
Beaumont
Philippeville

CHAPTER FIVE

THE BATTLE OF WATERLOO

The rain was still falling when dawn broke on Sunday, June 18th, and for men in both armies sleep had been almost impossible. Shortly after six, the English troops began to take up their positions and a mile away, across the valley, the French started to do likewise. Despite the somewhat pessimistic views of some of his generals, Napoleon was confident that victory would be his, and although news continued to arrive that the Prussians were marching towards Wavre—and therefore within reach of Wellington—he was still unwilling to believe that they were in any condition to take part in the battle.

At eleven o'clock, having despatched orders to Grouchy telling him to direct his movements upon Wavre so that he would be in a position not only to approach the main body of the French army but also to keep the Prussians away from the battlefield, Napoleon announced that he would launch a frontal attack, after which the rest of the army would exploit the gap in the English line. Such tactics were particularly unsuitable: Wellington, as usual, had chosen his ground well and the Emperor's plan would result in a high casualty rate.

The attack got under way shortly after eleven, with Napoleon feigning a diversion towards Hougoumont in the hope that the Duke would order some of his troops away from the centre of the line to strengthen his right. The idea misfired and for the first two hours the battle was centred around Hougoumont with Jérôme, the Emperor's brother, throwing in his infantry in an attempt to capture the buildings. Just before Napoleon intended to launch his main attack, a captured Prussian officer confirmed what his generals had suspected: Blücher had every intention of joining Wellington. More alarming than the news that Bülow's 1st Corps was marching towards them was the fact that Blücher, having assembled the rest of his army at Wavre, would be able to leave one corps in reserve whilst the bulk of his force advanced to link up with the English. But still Napoleon refused to believe what was now obvious, although, as a precautionary measure, he did despatch two divisions of cavalry to screen Bülow's path, deploying Lieutenant-General Count Lobau's 6th Corps behind them to hold back the Prussians until Grouchy was able to attack from the rear.

Around two o'clock, after an artillery barrage lasting about half an hour, four divisions of 18,000 men, commanded by Ney and d'Erlon, advanced towards Wellington's lines. But they went forward unprotected without any support from the cavalry and, to make matters worse, they were deployed in a totally impractical formation which increased their vulnerability and at the same time lessened their mobility. Nevertheless, they attacked with such resolution that for a while it very much looked as if the English line was on the point of collapse. They advanced to within forty yards of the enemy before the English opened a withering fire which was impossible to return, bringing the advance to a standstill. At last the French cavalry was seen to be coming up in support, but at that moment Lieutenant-General the Earl of Uxbridge decided to unleash his cavalry, overwhelming the French infantry and cuirassiers who supported them. The French broke ranks and retreated towards their lines, pursued by horsemen who rode them down as they went. But here matters got out of hand. The two cavalry brigades of Major-General Lord Edward Somerset (1st and 2nd Life Guards, Royal Horse Guards Blues and the 1st Dragoon Guards) and Major-General Sir William Ponsonby (1st Royal Dragoons, Royal Scots Greys and the 6th Inniskilling Dragoons) ignored Uxbridge's orders and charged so far forward that they were in turn overwhelmed by Napoleon's fresh cavalry and infantry, so that by the time they managed to extricate themselves, only one in three of the original force remained. Such foolhardiness had lost Wellington a quarter of his entire cavalry—2,500 men whom he could ill-afford to lose.

But at least the first crisis had been sufficiently overcome and for the moment the slopes in front of the English lines were clear of the enemy. Despite his losses, the advantage still remained with Wellington.

French troops advancing towards Hougoumont at the start of the battle

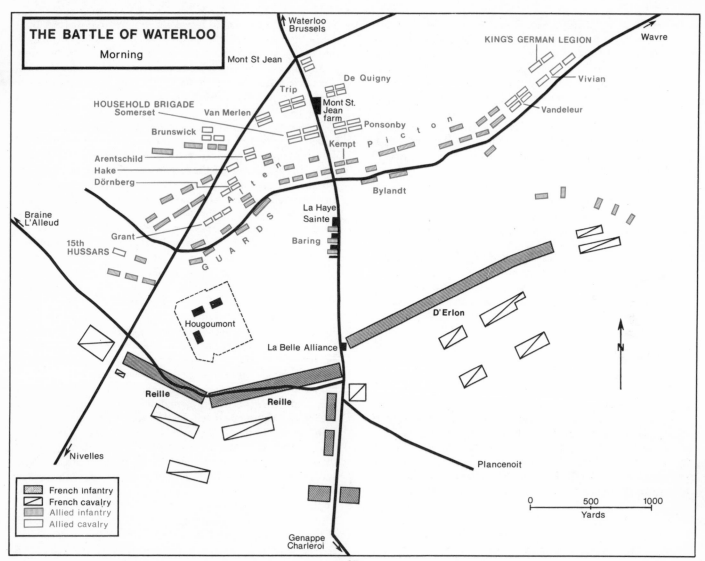

THE BATTLE OF WATERLOO
Morning

Waterloo
Brussels

KING'S GERMAN LEGION

Wavre

Mont St Jean

De Quigny

Vivian

Trip

Mont St.
Jean
farm

Vandeleur

HOUSEHOLD BRIGADE
Somerset

Van Merlen

Ponsonby

Picton

Brunswick

Kempt

Arentschild

Bylandt

Hake

Dörnberg

La Haye
Sainte

Braine
L'Alleud

Grant

Baring

15th
HUSSARS

GUARDS

Alten

D'Erlon

Hougoumont

N

La Belle Alliance

Reille

Reille

Nivelles

Plancenoit

	French infantry
	French cavalry
	Allied infantry
	Allied cavalry

0   500   1000
Yards

Genappe
Charleroi

27

When Grouchy's next despatch reached Napoleon, he was still nine miles from Wavre which meant that not only were the Prussians free to manoeuvre as they pleased but there was now no hope of the Marshal reaching the battlefield before nightfall. The Emperor realized that he was beginning to run short of time, for it was imperative that he defeat Wellington before Blücher arrived in force. Accordingly, he instructed Ney to seize La Haye Sainte, a farm which overlooked the centre of the English lines fortified as an outpost, as quickly as possible so that from this advanced point, a second assault could be mounted.

Incredibly, Ney decided to commit the greater part of his cavalry without any support from either infantry or artillery; the two battalions of infantry which he sent forward were soon repulsed although at one stage he even believed the English were falling back. He could not have been more mistaken: far from retreating, Wellington was actually strengthening his line. His men formed squares to meet Lieutenant-General Count Milhaud's cavalry charges and the gunners were ordered to take refuge inside them. From where Napoleon was watching, it appeared that Wellington's line had crumbled completely although the French cavalry, in spite of the fact that they had captured the majority of the English guns, had suffered appalling casualties and continued to do so as they rode around the squares. They were finally compelled to retreat when Lord Uxbridge ordered his cavalry forward, but quickly they reformed and returned to the attack.

Napoleon at least understood the folly of committing so large a portion of his cavalry to the field and he realized that if more were sent forward, there was a grave danger that the front would become so overcrowded that the whole impetus of the attack would be lost. Yet he had no hesitation in ordering Kellermann's divisions to follow and support Milhaud, and it was at this stage of the battle that the Prussians launched an assault against his right flank. The reaction of the English at witnessing more than 9,000 horsemen attacking a front of 1,000 yards was one of complete astonishment, but as far as Napoleon was concerned it was now imperative that Wellington be crushed as speedily as possible. Bülow's 1st Corps went into action shortly after four o'clock and almost immediately came under heavy fire from Lobau's 6th Corps. Blücher then transferred his assault to Lobau's right, at the same time receiving word that Lieutenant-General von Thielemann was under attack at Wavre.

Napoleon's position was deteriorating rapidly. Ney continued to order the cavalry forward without support and in so doing virtually destroyed the strongest arm of the French army. Only later, when the last cavalry charges were ended, did he send the infantry into action and since they, too, were unsupported, they stood no chance against the English gunners who, realizing that they were no longer threatened by the cavalry, were able to return to their posts.

Still La Haye Sainte remained uncaptured, but Napoleon now ordered that it be taken, no matter what the cost. And by that time, the defenders were beginning to run out of ammunition and Wellington had no more to send.

When the farm finally fell to the French, Ney was able to bring up a battery of horse artillery which, positioned only 300 yards away, wrought havoc along the English centre. The decisive hour of the battle had arrived. Wellington had almost exhausted his reserves and his line was weakening all the time. An attempt to counter-attack by Colonel Ompteda with two battalions of the King's German Legion met with no success, and a number of other formations collapsed completely. Although Wellington's left was holding firm, his right was being seriously threatened and the casualty list, particularly among the senior officers, was mounting considerably. But if the Duke's centre was weakening, Ney at least did not have sufficient troops to call up from reserve to renew the assault which could well have resulted in the total collapse of the English line. Had he not wasted his reserves by a series of futile attacks mounted throughout the afternoon, the outcome of the battle might well have been very different. A request to Napoleon for reinforcements was denied, despite the fact that the Emperor had fourteen battalions of his best infantry still waiting to go into action. Such a denial must remain a mystery, for Napoleon could not have been unaware of the critical state the battle had now reached. Even though the Prussians had driven his troops out of Plancenoit on his right flank and were threatening his rear, he must have realized that unless Ney overcame the English within the next fifteen minutes the likelihood of victory was virtually over. But instead of assisting Ney, he decided to strengthen his right by sending two battalions of the Old Guard to recover Plancenoit. This they did, by which time Wellington had been given a vital half-hour to reorganize his defences so that when Napoleon next turned his attention to the main front, he discovered that Ziethen had arrived to reinforce the centre of the English line. At last he decided to release the Guard to carry the English front, but it was too late; the appearance of fresh troops before them did much to dishearten the exhausted French infantry and they began to fall back, even though the Guard was

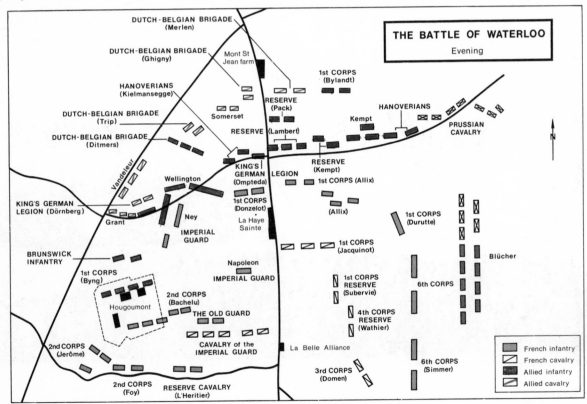

THE BATTLE OF WATERLOO
Evening

DUTCH-BELGIAN BRIGADE
(Merlen)

DUTCH-BELGIAN BRIGADE
(Ghigny)

Mont St
Jean farm

1st CORPS
(Bylandt)

HANOVERIANS
(Kielmansegge)

RESERVE
(Pack)

HANOVERIANS

DUTCH-BELGIAN BRIGADE
(Trip)

Somerset

Kempt

PRUSSIAN
CAVALRY

DUTCH-BELGIAN BRIGADE
(Ditmers)

RESERVE (Lambert)

RESERVE
(Kempt)

Vandeleur

KING'S
GERMAN LEGION
(Ompteda)

Wellington

1st CORPS (Allix)

KING'S GERMAN
LEGION (Dörnberg)

1st CORPS
(Donzelot)

(Allix)

1st CORPS
(Durutte)

Grant

Ney

La Haye
Sainte

1st CORPS
(Jacquinot)

IMPERIAL
GUARD

Blücher

6th CORPS

BRUNSWICK
INFANTRY

Napoleon

1st CORPS
RESERVE
(Subervie)

1st CORPS
(Byng)

IMPERIAL GUARD

Hougoumont

2nd CORPS
(Bachelu)

4th CORPS
RESERVE
(Wathier)

THE OLD GUARD

2nd CORPS
(Jerôme)

La Belle Alliance

6th CORPS
(Simmer)

CAVALRY of the
IMPERIAL GUARD

French infantry

French cavalry

2nd CORPS
(Foy)

RESERVE CAVALRY
(L'Heritier)

3rd CORPS
(Domen)

Allied infantry

Allied cavalry

29

coming up in support. Further reinforcements met the Guard's counter-attack, who came forward under heavy artillery fire, fighting their way into the English lines where they met volley after volley of musket fire. Confusion grew rife as their officers tried to deploy them, and immediately Wellington ordered the charge. The French suffered terrible casualties which were impossible to sustain so that again they were forced to retreat. Such an occurrence signalled that the battle was lost; a wholesale withdrawal was under way.

Wellington ordered a general advance in pursuit and as more and more positions were overrun, the last organized resistance came to an end. Vainly, Napoleon endeavoured to reform the Guard in an attempt to stem the rout but in the confusion he was forced to order their retreat. Shortly after Wellington and Blücher met at La Belle Alliance, the defeated Emperor reached Genappe to learn that there was no way open to him to mount a final stand.

The Battle of Waterloo was over.

French cavalry attacking British squares

CHAPTER SIX

THE MEN

Corporal of the 42nd (the Black Watch) and Private of the 92nd (the Gordon Highlanders)

Infantrymen and Private of the 3rd Hussars, King's German Legion

Any comparison made between Wellington and Napoleon reveals that no two men could have been more diametrically opposite than they, for whilst Wellington was a backbone of the establishment which had nurtured him all his life, Napoleon was against any system that was not of his own design. The troops under Wellington's command respected him but they did not love him. The worst crime a soldier could commit in his estimation was to fail in his duty and bravery was part of that duty. He respected the infantry above all other units in the army and he went to infinite trouble to protect it. But if he had to fight an enemy, he also had to fight Parliament: risk was a necessary hazard which had to be taken in war and he knew that the retention of his command rested not only on victory but avoiding a drain on his manpower. He was reluctant to delegate power: he kept a strong rein on his troops and if strict discipline was responsible for the unhesitating obedience of his men, so, too, was the care he afforded them. They knew he did all he could to see they were paid promptly and quartered comfortably, and from this stemmed their respect.

Napoleon, in comparison, was worshipped by the men that served under him. He had a magic quality about him which was impossible to resist, even though he treated them badly and left them, after his defeat in Egypt and Russia, to make their own way back to France. In the early days of his career his victories came from skill and daring, but latterly, when he handed over the command to others, he asked for only one thing: victory, at any price. He squandered his men, often deploying them in a way which although might win victory took a heavy toll on life. And yet, despite all this, he was loved and able to rely on his army's faith in him at all times.

It was under the command of these two men that the Battle of Waterloo was fought. Possibly the greatest difference between the two armies was in the recruitment of their officers for whilst, following the disappearance of many of the French noble families in the Revolution, the majority of Napoleon's officers were commissioned from the ranks, their English counterparts obtained their commissions by wealth and birth. Instances of advancement through merit were rare: vacancies caused by death or injury in battle were filled by promotion within the regiment so that if an officer had little wealth and was unfortunate enough to serve in a regiment which saw only infrequent action, promotion was a long time in coming. Commissioning from the ranks was not as rare as might be supposed but advancement beyond the rank of captain or major was virtually impossible if the soldier was without private means. Perhaps the most surprising fact of this system of purchase was that it worked at all. Far from being incompetent, as might be supposed, the English army was generally regarded—even by the French—to contain some of the best officers of the day.

The rank and file of the army was looked on by Wellington as 'infamous', made up of criminals and ne'er-do-wells who, despite the hardships which existed, were probably better off than their civilian counterparts. Their loyalty to their regiments was undeniable; there existed a common bond of friendship between officers and men alike, and the lack of resentment at the privileges afforded to one man as opposed to another was largely the result of the class structure of the time.

A sergeant received thirteen pence a day, sixpence of which was deducted to meet the cost of his food. This, taken together with various other benefits, compared favourably with the weekly wage of a labourer at home, and on retirement he might receive a pension of ninepence a day, threepence more than a private. At the end of a campaign, troops might be awarded a lump sum as prize money—after Waterloo, sergeants received about twenty pounds each (Wellington, as Commander-in-Chief, got sixty-one thousand pounds). Much of a soldier's pay was spent on tobacco and drink; looting and pillaging—an accepted practice in the French army—was strongly opposed by Wellington.

The French infantry were certainly more adaptable in the

field than the English; Napoleon's habit of not concerning himself with their quartering resulted in them having a greater ability in the construction of bivouacs and making the most of whatever material was to hand. Pay was erratic which was largely the cause of much of the plundering which occurred after a successful battle.

By far the most glamorous arm of any army was the cavalry. Decked in highly flamboyant and colourful uniforms, its purpose was to screen and to observe, to maintain the lines of communication, to pursue and to crush infantry which had been weakened by artillery and hand-to-hand fighting. The light cavalry was used to assess the position and manoeuvres of the enemy. It was the heavy brigade whose job it was to overcome and cripple the infantry. At the first sign of a cavalry attack, infantry would immediately form into squares and the artillery would take shelter within them. Depending on their size, the lines of troops might be two or three deep, the second firing over the heads of the first whilst they were reloading. It was customary and necessary for cannon to remain in position which inevitably resulted in its capture—if the cavalry was repulsed then it was left to the infantry to retake the ground it had lost so that the gunners could take up their posts once more. But if there was safety in the square formation, there was danger as well: the cavalry only had to give the impression that they were about to charge and the infantry would regroup; they would then hold off and the squares would be subjected to a heavy artillery bombardment which would inflict a heavy loss of life.

ROYAL HORSE ARTILLERY.

Gunner of the Royal Horse Artillery

Private of the 2nd, Royal North British Dragoons, (the Scots Greys). The figure in the background is wearing service uniform

CHAPTER SEVEN

THE WEAPONS

The muskets with which the infantry were equipped at Waterloo were substantially the same in all three armies. Smooth-bored and weighing between ten and fourteen pounds, they had altered little in the last hundred years. Their length averaged about fifty-five inches and the bayonet added a further fifteen when fitted in the socket outside the barrel. It was possible for well-trained troops to fire at the rate of about twice a minute, but only for a certain length of time. The Brown Bess, with which the English were equipped, needed to be washed out every hundred rounds and new flints inserted; the cartridge, which was made by hand and was waxed in order to prevent damp, had to be cut or torn open and a small quantity of powder sprinkled into the firing pan. The rest of the powder was poured down the muzzle, together with the ball and a piece of wadding, all of which had to be packed tight with a ramrod. When the trigger was pulled, the spark from the flint would catch the powder in the pan which in turn would ignite the main charge in the barrel. Assuming that the loading operation had been carried out correctly (and it was easy to go wrong when the enemy was continuing to advance the whole time), the percentage of misfires was still about one in five; the ball itself could inflict injury up to a range of about 500 yards but a hit at this distance was purely accidental. More often, the effective range was in the region of seventy-five yards.

The Green Jackets: Riflemen of the 60th (which did not take part in the battle) and the 95th (which was equipped with the Baker Rifle)

Waterloo Cannon

36

The Brown Bess

The artillery comprised, in the main, four-, eight- and twelve-pounders and in addition howitzers and mortars were also used. The English army even had a rocket troop but it was the cannon which played the major role. There was no mechanism to absorb the recoil and after each round had been fired the gun had to be reloaded. Nevertheless, it was possible for skilled artillery to fire, clean the muzzle, reload and fire again within half a minute. A constant watch had to be kept on the enemy cavalry; there was no chance of survival at all if a gunner happened to be caught in a cavalry charge and cannon were continually being taken and retaken in battle.

British cavalry consisted of the Household Cavalry, Dragoons, Light Dragoons and Hussars; the French of Cuirassiers, Chasseurs, Carabiniers, Dragoons, Hussars, Horse Grenadiers and Lancers. (There were no Lancers in the British army until four Light Dragoon regiments were converted to the new arm in 1816–17.) With this exception, their arms and equipment were virtually the same. British Heavy Cavalry used a straight sword which was thirty-five inches long with a flat guard in the form of a disc pierced with round holes; Light Cavalry was armed with a stirrup-hilted sword with a curved blade which measured just over thirty-two inches from shoulder to point. The 1796-pattern Light Dragoon pistol—a flintlock weapon with a short, rounded butt—was still in general use, and Royal Horse Artillery gunners were equipped with a double-barrelled side-by-side pistol.

Belgian infantry of the Dutch-Belgian Army

FIRST REGIMENT of LIFE GUARDS.

A PRIVATE of the 13th LIGHT DRAGOONS.

Privates of the 1st Regiment of Life Guards (Heavy Cavalry) and the 13th Light Dragoons (Light Cavalry)

38

CHAPTER EIGHT

AFTERMATH

The Battle of Waterloo

Napoleon was beaten. He had finally given up all hope of being able to muster what remained of his army to make one last stand, and he now concentrated on reaching Paris as quickly as possible in order to forestall the intriguing which he was sure was taking place. He reached the Elysée on the morning of June 21st, but he knew his position to be an impossible one. Although he still commanded a surprising degree of support from the people, the politicians were no longer prepared to go along with him and there was a danger that civil war would break out. Resistance against the Allied armies was out of the question and it was certain that the coalition governments were not going to allow him to remain on the throne. And so, on the day following his return, he abdicated for the second time, in favour of his young son, and soon after left Paris for ever. It was hoped that he might be able to escape to America where many who fought in his army were to settle, but when he was about to make good his escape he discovered that the ports were blockaded and instead was forced to surrender to Captain Maitland of the *Bellerophon*. Within days he was sailing towards St Helena in the Atlantic where he was to spend the rest of his life in exile.

With the defeat of Napoleon, the war which had been waged almost continuously since 1793 came to an end. No longer was Europe threatened by a dictator whose armies had subdued one nation after another, who had won victory after victory in his quest for power. News of the victory at Waterloo was carried to England by Wellington's aide-de-camp, Major the Hon H. Percy, and published in *The Times* on Thursday, June 22nd. Wellington's despatch was addressed to Earl Bathurst, Principal Secretary of State for the War Department, and he began by relating the events which took place before the 18th. He then went on to give a brief description of the battle itself before continuing: 'Your Lordship will observe, that such a desperate action could not be fought, and such advantage could not be gained, without great loss; and I am sorry to add that ours has been immense . . .

'It gives me the greatest satisfaction to assure your Lordship,

that the army never, upon any occasion, conducted itself better . . . and there is no Officer, nor description of troops, that did not behave well . . .

'I should not do justice to my feelings or to Marshal Blücher and the Prussian army, if I did not attribute the successful result of this arduous day, to the cordial and timely assistance I received from them . . .'

It was left to the Prussians to pursue the retreating French forces and only the 6th Corps of General Lobau were to reach Paris in a condition which might conceivably have assisted Napoleon further. Honours were heaped upon Wellington who was to remain in command of the Occupation Army for a further three years before returning to England to re-enter political life. Louis XVIII returned to France as king, one hundred days exactly after he had left. He died in 1824, three years after Napoleon, five after Blücher. Wellington lived on for another twenty-eight.

The Battle of Waterloo has never been forgotten. Today, it is commemorated by both English and French alike. Its triumph has been kept alive by the memories of those who took part, for whom nothing ever replaced its glory.

The Anglo-Allied Army

Commander-in-Chief	*Field-Marshal the Duke of Wellington*
Chief of the Staff	*Colonel Sir William Howe de Lancey, KB*
Adjutant-General	*Major-General Sir E. Barnes, KB*
Commanding Royal Artillery	*Colonel Sir G. Wood*
Commanding Engineer	*Lieutenant-Colonel Smyth*
Prussian Attaché	*Major-General Baron von Müffling*

1st CORPS

Commander	*The Prince of Orange*
Commander, 1st Division	*Major-General Cooke*
Brigades:	*Major-General Maitland*
	Major-General Sir John Byng
Artillery:	*Lieutenant-Colonel Adye*
Commander, 3rd Division	*Lieutenant-General Count Sir Charles Alten*
Brigades:	*Major-General Sir Colin Halkett*
	Colonel Baron von Ompteda
	Major-General Count Kielmansegge

Artillery:	*Lieutenant-Colonel Williamson*
Commander, 2nd Dutch-Belgian Division	*Lieutenant-General Baron de Perponcher*
Brigades:	*Major-General Count de Bylandt*
	Prince Bernard of Saxe-Weimar
Artillery:	*Major Van Opstal*
Commander, 3rd Dutch-Belgian Division	*Lieutenant-General Baron Chassè*
Brigades:	*Major-General Ditmers*
	Major-General d'Aubreme
Artillery:	*Major van der Smissen*

2nd CORPS

Commander	*Lieutenant-General Lord Hill*
Commander, 2nd Division	*Lieutenant-General Sir Henry Clinton*
Brigades:	*Major-General Adam*
	Colonel du Plat
	Colonel Halkett
Artillery:	*Lieutenant-Colonel Gold*
Commander, 4th Division	*Lieutenant-General Sir Charles Colville*
Brigades:	*Colonel Mitchell*
	Major-General Johnstone
	Major-General Sir James Lyon
Artillery:	*Lieutenant-Colonel Hawker*

2nd CORPS (cont.)

Corps of Prince Frederick
of the Netherlands:

Commander, 1st Dutch-Belgian Division	*Lieutenant-General Stedman*
Brigades:	*Major-General d'Hauw*
	Major-General d'Eerens

Commander, Netherland Indian Brigade	*Lieutenant-General Anthing*

RESERVE

Commander	*Field-Marshal the Duke of Wellington*
Commander, 5th Division	*Lieutenant-General Sir Thomas Picton*
Brigades:	*Major-General Sir James Kempt*
	Major-General Sir Denis Pack
	Colonel von Wincke
Artillery:	*Major Heisse*
Commander, 6th Division	*Lieutenant-General, the Hon Sir Lowry Cole*
Brigades:	*Major-General Sir John Lambert*
	Colonel Best
Artillery:	*Lieutenant-Colonel Brückmann*
Commander, British Reserve Artillery	*Major Drummond*
Commander, Brunswick Corps	*The Duke of Brunswick*
Commander, Nassau Contingent	*General von Kruse*

CAVALRY

Commander	*Lieutenant-General the Earl of Uxbridge*
Brigades:	*Major-General Lord Edward Somerset*
	Major-General Sir William Ponsonby
	Major-General Sir William Dornberg
	Major-General Sir John Vandeleur
	Major-General Sir Colquhoun Grant
	Major-General Sir Hussey Vivian
	Colonel Baron von Arentschildt
Commander, British Horse Artillery Troops	*Lieutenant-Colonel Sir Augustus Fraser*
Commander, 1st Hanoverian Cavalry Brigade	*Colonel von Estorff*
Commander, Dutch-Belgian Cavalry Division	*Lieutenant-General Baron de Collaert*

Officers and men of the Imperial Guard

The Prussian Guard:
Line infantry and Jagers

Prussian cavalry

List of Anglo-Allied Army Regiments and Units

1st CORPS

1st Division — 2nd and 3rd battalions, 1st Guards; 2nd battalion, 2nd Guards; 2nd battalion, 3rd Guards

  Artillery: Captain Sandham's Field Brigade, RA; Major Kühlmann's Horse Artillery Troop, King's German Legion

3rd Division — 2nd battalion, 30th; 33rd (Duke of Wellington's); 2nd battalion, 69th; 2nd battalion, 73rd; 1st and 2nd Light Battalions and 5th and 8th Line Battalions, King's German Legion; 6 Hanoverian battalions

  Artillery: Major Lloyd's Field Brigade, RA; Captain Cleeves' Field Brigade, King's German Legion

2nd Dutch-Belgian Division — 5 Dutch-Belgian battalions; 5 Nassau battalions

  Artillery: Bijleveld's Horse Battery; 1 Field Battery

3rd Dutch-Belgian Division — 12 Dutch-Belgian battalions

  Artillery: 1 Horse and 1 Field Battery

2nd CORPS

2nd Division — 1st battalion, 52nd; 1st battalion, 71st; 2nd and 3rd battalions, 95th; 1st, 2nd, 3rd and 4th Line Battalions, King's German Legion; 4 Landwehr (Hanoverian) battalions

  Artillery: Captain Bolton's Field Brigade, RA; Major Sympher's Horse Artillery Troops, King's German Legion

4th Division — 3rd battalion, 14th; 1st battalion, 23rd; 51st; 2nd battalion, 35th; 1st battalion, 54th; 2nd battalion, 59th; 1st battalion, 91st; 5 Hanoverian battalions

  Artillery: Major Brome's Field Brigade, RA; Captain von Rettberg's Hanoverian Field Battery

1st Dutch-Belgian Division — 11 battalions

Netherland Indian Brigade — 5 battalions

  Artillery: 1 Field Battery

RESERVE

5th Division — 1st battalion, 28th; 1st battalion, 32nd; 1st battalion, 79th; 1st battalion, 95th; 3rd battalion, 1st; 1st battalion, 42nd; 2nd battalion, 44th; 1st battalion, 92nd; 4 Landwehr (Hanoverian) battalions

  Artillery: Major Rogers' Field Brigade, RA; Captain Braun's Hanoverian Field Battery

6th Division — 1st battalion, 4th; 1st battalion, 27th; 1st battalion, 40th; 2nd battalion, 81st; 4 Landwehr (Hanoverian) battalions.

  Artillery: Major Unett's Field Brigade, RA; Captain Sinclair's Field Brigade, RA

British Reserve Artillery — 2 Horse Artillery Troops; 3 companies, RA

Brunswick Corps — Advanced Guard; 4 companies of infantry; 1 cavalry detachment; 2 brigades (6 battalions); 2 batteries.

Nassau Contingent — 3 battalions

Anglo-Allied Army Regiments and Units (cont.)

GARRISONS

7th Division	*7th British Brigade: 2nd battalion, 25th; 2nd battalion, 37th; 2nd battalion, 78th; 3 British Garrison battalions*
Hanoverian Reserve Corps	*12 Landwehr battalions in 4 Brigades*

CAVALRY

	1st and 2nd Life Guards; Royal Horse Guards Blues; 1st Dragoon Guards; 1st Royal Dragoons; Royal Scots Greys; 6th Inniskilling Dragoons; 1st and 2nd Light Dragoons, King's German Legion; 23rd Light Dragoons; 11th, 12th and 16th Light Dragoons; 7th and 15th Hussars; 2nd Hussars, King's German Legion; 10th and 18th Hussars; 1st Hussars, King's German Legion; 13th Light Dragoons; 3rd Hussars, King's German Legion
British Horse Artillery Troops (attached to cavalry)	*Major Bull's Troop (howitzers); Lieutenant-Colonel Webber-Smith's Troop; Lieutenant-Colonel Sir R. Gardiner's Troop; Major E.C. Whinyates' Troop (with rockets); Major Norman Ramsay's Troop; Captain Mercer's Troop*
1st Hanoverian Cavalry Brigade	*3 regiments: Prince Regent's Hussars; Bremen and Vereen Hussars; Cumberland Hussars*
Brunswick Cavalry	*1 regiment of Hussars; 1 squadron of Uhlans*
Dutch-Belgian Cavalry Division	*3 brigades*
Artillery:	*2 half horse batteries*

The Prussian Army

Commander-in-Chief	*Field-Marshal Prince Blücher von Wahlstadt*
Quartermaster-General and Chief of the Staff	*General Count von Gneisenau*
Chief of the General Staff	*General von Grölmann*
1st CORPS	
Commander Brigades:	*Lieutenant-General von Ziethen* *Major-General von Steinmetz* *Major-General von Pirch II*
Brigades: (cont.)	*Major-General von Jagow* *Major-General Count von Henckel Donnersmarck*
Commander, Cavalry Corps Brigades:	*Lieutenant-General von Röder* *Major-General von Treskow* *Lieutenant-Colonel von Lützow*
Artillery:	*Colonel von Lehmann*
2nd CORPS	
Commander	*Major-General von Pirch I*

The Prussian Army (cont.)

Brigades:	Major-General von Tippelskirch	Commander, Cavalry Corps	General von Hobe
	Major-General von Kraft	Brigades:	Colonel von der Marwitz
	Major-General von Brause		Colonel Count von Lottum
	Major-General von Bose	Artillery:	Colonel von Mohnhaupt

4th CORPS

Commander, Cavalry Corps	Major-General von Wahlen-Jurgass	Commander	General Count Bülow von Dennewitz
Brigades:	Colonel von Thümen	Brigades:	Lieutenant-General von Hacke
	Colonel Count von Schulenburg		General von Ryssel
	Lieutenant-Colonel von Sohr		General von Losthin
Artillery:	Colonel von Röhl		Colonel von Hiller

3rd CORPS

Commander	Lieutenant-General von Thielemann	Commander, Cavalry Corps	General Prince William of Prussia
Brigades:	Major-General von Borcke	Brigades:	General von Sidow
	Colonel von Kämpfen		Colonel Count von Schwerin
	Colonel von Luck		Lieutenant-Colonel von Watsdorf
	Colonel von Stülpnägel	Artillery:	Lieutenant-Colonel von Bardeleben

The French Army

Commander-in-Chief	The Emperor Napoleon	Commander, 3rd Division	Lieutenant-General Baron Marcognet
		Commander, 4th Division	Lieutenant-General Count Durutte
Chief of the Staff	Marshal Soult, Duke of Dalmatia		
		Commander, Cavalry Division	Lieutenant-General Baron Jacquinot
Commander of Artillery	Lieutenant-General Ruty		
Commander of Engineers	Lieutenant-General Baron Roginiat	Commander, Artillery	Baron de Salles

1st CORPS

2nd CORPS

Commander	Lieutenant-General Count Drouet d'Erlon	Commander	Lieutenant-General Count Reille
Commander, 1st Division	Lieutenant-General Allix	Commander, 5th Division	Lieutenant-General Baron Bachelu
Commander, 2nd Division	Lieutenant-General Baron Donzelot	Commander, 6th Division	Lieutenant-General Prince Jérôme Bonaparte

The French Army (cont.)

Commander, 7th Division	*Lieutenant-General Count Girard*
Commander, 9th Division	*Lieutenant-General Count Foy*
Commander, 2nd Cavalry Division	*Lieutenant-General Baron Pire*
Commander, Artillery	*Baron Pellitier*

3rd CORPS

Commander	*Lieutenant-General Count Vandamme*
Commander, 8th Division	*Lieutenant-General Baron Lefol*
Commander, 10th Division	*Lieutenant-General Baron Habert*
Commander, 11th Division	*Lieutenant-General Baron Berthézène*
Commander, 3rd Cavalry Division	*Lieutenant-General Baron Domon*
Commander, Artillery	*General Doguereau*

4th CORPS

Commander	*Lieutenant-General Count Gérard*
Commander, 12th Division	*Lieutenant-General Baron Pécheux*
Commander, 13th Division	*Lieutenant-General Baron Vichery*
Commander, 14th Division	*Lieutenant-General de Bourmont/ General Hulot*
Commander, 7th Cavalry Division	*Lieutenant-General Maurin*
Commander, Artillery	*General Baron Baltus*

6th CORPS

Commander	*Lieutenant-General Count Lobau*
Commander, 19th Division	*Lieutenant-General Baron Simmer*
Commander, 20th Division	*Lieutenant-General Baron Jeannin*
Commander, 21st Division	*Lieutenant-General Baron Teste*
Commander, Artillery	*Lieutenant-General Baron Noury*

RESERVE CAVALRY

Commander	*Marshal Count de Grouchy*

1st CORPS

Commander	*Lieutenant-General Count Pajol*
Commander, 4th Division	*Lieutenant-General Baron Soult*
Commander, 5th Division	*Lieutenant-General Baron Subervie*

2nd CORPS

Commander	*Lieutenant-General Count Exelmans*
Commander, 9th Division	*Lieutenant-General Baron Strolz*
Commander, 10th Division	*Lieutenant-General Chastel*

3rd CORPS

Commander	*Lieutenant-General Kellermann, Count Valmy*
Commander, 11th Division	*Lieutenant-General Baron L'heritier*
Commander, 12th Division	*Lieutenant-General Roussel d'Hurbal*

4th CORPS

Commander	*Lieutenant-General Count Milhaud*
Commander, 13th Division	*Lieutenant-General Wathier de St Alphonse*
Commander, 14th Division	*Lieutenant-General Baron Delort*

THE IMPERIAL GUARD

Commander	*Marshal Mortier, Duke of Treviso*
Aide-Major-General de la Garde	*Lieutenant-General Count Drouot*
Division Commanders	*Lieutenant-General Count Friant*
	Lieutenant-General Count Morand
	Lieutenant-General Count Duhesme

Strength of the Armies

ANGLO-ALLIED ARMY				
1st Corps:	25,200	men	56	guns
2nd Corps:	24,000	men	40	guns
Reserve:	20,500	men	64	guns
Garrison:	12,200	men		
Cavalry:	14,500	men		
Miscellaneous:	1,200	men		
Total:	97,600	men	160	guns

PRUSSIAN ARMY				
1st Corps:	31,100	men	80	guns
2nd Corps:	31,500	men	80	guns
3rd Corps:	24,150	men	48	guns
4th Corps:	30,050	men	88	guns
Total:	116,800	men	296	guns

FRENCH ARMY				
1st Corps:	20,700	men	46	guns
2nd Corps:	25,200	men	46	guns
3rd Corps:	18,100	men	38	guns
4th Corps:	15,400	men	38	guns
6th Corps:	10,800	men	38	guns
Reserve Cavalry:	13,150	men	48	guns
Total:	103,350*	men	254	guns

*This figure excludes the Imperial Guard